Making Scripture Yours

David R. Mains

David C. Cook Publishing Co.

ELGIN, ILLINOIS—WESTON, ONTARIO

MAKING SCRIPTURE YOURS
©1980 David R. Mains

All Scripture quotations are from the Revised Standard Version unless otherwise noted.

Published by David C. Cook Publishing Co., Elgin, IL 60120
Cover design by Joe Ragont
Printed in the United States of America.
ISBN 0-89191-272-x
LC 80-51284

CONTENTS

The Chapel Talks Series by David Mains

Introduction

Most people listen to the radio while they're doing something else. As a broadcaster I'm aware that a person hearing me is probably shaving, fixing breakfast, driving to work, or some similar activity. Being able to keep his or her attention in such a setting is a lot different than preaching to a captive audience.

Therefore, I was dubious as to whether the slow pace of radio with its need for frequent repetition and underscoring each key truth would transfer all that well into print.

To complicate matters further, every time a program is made I must assume many listeners didn't hear what was said the day before. But just the opposite is true when compiling the chapters of a book. They build on one another.

Well, the first series of Chapel talks is now completed. Through the help of others, my broadcast scripts have been made more readable than I thought possible. The greatest thanks for this project goes to my wife, Karen, who put aside her own writing to help me out. Two Chapel of the Air staff members, Ruby Christian and Sharon Morse, also did yeoman duty typing long hours after work and on weekends.

1
THE MYSTERY OF SCRIPTURE

The saying "Familiarity breeds contempt" comes from Aesop's account of an unwise fox who foolishly forgot how impressed he was the first time he saw a great lion. In other words, intimacy has a tendency to lessen our appreciation of something.

Certainly this was the flaw that plagued the nation of Israel throughout its early history, as recorded in the Old Testament. The honor of being God's chosen people, of seeing him work great miracles on their behalf, of knowing his laws because he had literally revealed his thoughts to them—all this was frequently taken for granted. The narrative too often describes Israel as despising her great privileges.

Intellectually, the people knew that the favors accorded them were extraordinary, but this awareness didn't necessarily affect how they lived. They saw, but not really. They believed, but not truly. Their obvious casualness toward the things of God rarely bothered them. This was especially prevalent among those several generations removed from great revelations or from leaders of special repute or from unusual manifestations of God.

That's why the Lord established festivals to commemorate such times. He commanded his leaders to erect monuments at sites where he had demonstrated his care in outstanding ways. He had written down what he was continually doing so people wouldn't forget or overlook the magnificent honor accorded them of being recipients of his overtures.

Their forefathers, such as the patriarchs, were to be highly respected. The memory of how God rewarded their faith was to be passed on from generation to generation. The Israelites were to understand that much of the goodness they experienced was because of God's promises to these earlier people.

But surely we Christians today can't be faulted for failing to appreciate God's revelation of himself to us, can we? Or is it possible we evidence those same symptoms?

Let's look at one obvious way God continues to make himself known in our present world. Paul wrote to Timothy, "All Scripture is inspired by God" (2 Tim. 3:16). Writing on the same topic Peter said, "Men moved by the Holy Spirit spoke from God" (2 Pet. 1:21). Although the Bible and God are not equal, the Lord has tied himself to his Word in a special way.

How marvelous to live in a day when we're able to read freely from a book containing the very thoughts of

God himself. In fact, if he were to speak aloud his current desires, thundering forth what he wanted us to know, I sincerely doubt that he would share anything not already contained in the Scriptures. God has done his part in making available to us everything we need to know about life—past, present, and future.

Fellow human beings have played a large role in this miracle as well. The history of the English Bible includes the stories of men like John Wycliffe, who in the 1300's was burdened to place the Scriptures in the hands of the common man. This was long before Luther's 95 Theses or the invention of the printing press.

The opposition was intense. Wycliffe was soon sending out his followers as poor traveling preachers who went throughout the land with handwritten copies of parts of the Bible in the language of the people. In your imagination you can almost see the secretive scenes. Here a farmer quickly exchanges several bags of turnips for two chapters of Romans. There a load of hay is delivered on a back road for parts of a Gospel. Though he was despised and eventually excommunicated by the church, we owe much to this one called "the Morning Star of the Reformation."

Then there was William Tyndale. His translation appeared almost one hundred-fifty years later. His earthly reward for this monumental work was to be strangled before being burned at the stake. His last words, as a young man still in his early forties, were, "Lord, open the King of England's eyes."

It's great to have three or four Bibles in our homes. But it wasn't always that way. Even today there are stories of sacrifice so others may know God's thoughts in their own language. Missionaries and translators die in foreign lands because of disease or persecution or overwork. Just because we happen to be generations removed from godly forebears who risked their lives doesn't give us the right to treat our privilege casually. Rather, the availability of God's Word ought to fill our hearts with deep gratitude.

"Agreed," you say. "But I'm a little reluctant to equate a mere lack of respect for a book with Old Testament Israel's sins. I mean, they were blessed with outright miracles: the sea parting, a pillar of fire and a cloud to lead them, Jericho's walls falling down, and similar spectacles."

"That's right," I respond. "But don't forget that God also revealed himself through the prophets and through the Law and, of course, through his Son. In each case, and even with Christ (who did many signs and wonders, healed the sick, and even raised the dead), the people didn't remember how impressed they were. They forgot the wonder they felt when they first heard the Commandments or experienced the thundering voice of an Elijah, or watched the gentle Teacher on a Galilean hillside. "Seeing, they do not see," said Jesus.

"How can you be God and a man as well?" they asked.

I don't know, but he was 100 percent of each—100 percent human and 100 percent divine. It's a mystery, this living Word.

Can our faith be exercised in similar fashion when it comes to the written word? It is of God and it is of man, divine and human. Not 75 percent supernatural and 25 percent natural, or the reverse. But 100 percent of each, totally divine and totally human. Neither side of this mystery can be minimized. This book is like no other volume in all the world, and it is to be handled with the utmost respect.

Psalm 119 with 176 verses is about the Scriptures. I like verse 18 very much: "Open my eyes, that I may behold wondrous things out of thy law" (v. 18). If I paraphrase the sentence it represents the thrust of what I want to say: *Open eyes behold the wonder of God's Word.*

My desire for you, good friend, is that your eyes might always be open to see the magnificence of the Bible, that you might behold its wonder. I desire that you would again marvel regarding what God has given you in his written Word.

In Christian art, paintings of Christ or of a saint usually had a ring of light surrounding the head. In reality Jesus didn't have a halo—nor did any of his followers, for that matter, though I imagine it could do wonders for a person's ego to suddenly be granted one. If I were a recipient, I know I'd make it a point to walk outside at night so that my neighbors could get the full effect of my illumined saintliness against the evening sky. In art such a technique made certain the viewer would not miss anyone who was especially holy in a given painting.

Now my desire is to help you put a permanent halo around God's Word. The following prayer is a start. My hope is that you will keep a copy of it in the front of your Bible and every time you read God's Word, you would refer to the prayer and say:

Father, once again I want to exercise my privilege of

learning your thoughts as revealed in this marvelous book, the Bible. In the moments ahead, please help me to remember that I hold a miracle in my hand.

Thank you for the various roles played by faithful fellow human beings that have afforded me this opportunity. I also give praise to you, God, not only because you by nature are truth, but in a manner beyond my ability to comprehend you make your truth wonderfully known through these unique writings.

Never do I want to take what is in these pages for granted. I know many brothers and sisters in Christ don't have the Scriptures available to them, and there's no reason I should deserve this opportunity more than they. Please know that I appreciate the tremendous privilege of being able to read freely from this sacred volume.

Help me to be as attentive to learning from your written word as I would be were the LIVING WORD to come and instruct me. With open eyes I once again come to behold the wonder of your book.

Amen.

I hope these words will enable you to approach the Scriptures with a sense of wonder. You see, God's Word was never intended to be picked up and read like a newspaper. That's why I wrote the prayer. You need to make use of it over and over until the proper mind-set becomes an integral part of you.

2
MEDITATING

"Are you a social misfit? Do you envy those who seem to know precisely what to say and exactly how to act? Well, read the *Art of Knowing Who You Are and What You're Supposed to Be When Other People Are Around,* a book by a world authority on charm, Princess Luciabelli, and discover yourself becoming a person of great magnetism."

Have you ever seen advertisements of this type? What would you say to someone noted for his abrasive ways and lack of tact if he said, "Don't bodder me right now. I got dese tree more chapters t'read before I become 'charmin.'"

"What do you mean?" you ask.

"Dis ad says dat if I jest read dis book, I'll be transformed overnight into a charmin' poersin. Now get outta here already. I only gotta couple chapters more."

Would you attempt to explain that it's all a little more

complex than that? "Sir, the key isn't in just reading it. Rather, the ideas have to be applied over a period of time. Why, your expectations are not really . . ."

"Hey, you, you're boddering me. I'm almost done."

As strange as it may sound, sometimes I feel this is the same mind-set a lot of people bring to the study of God's Word. They want to become spiritually mature, and this is good. They correctly see that the Scriptures play a major role in achieving this desire. But for some reason, they think that reading is the key when actually another word is far more important.

In contrast to merely reading the Bible we need to develop the discipline of meditating on it. In the last chapter we discussed the need to marvel regarding the Scriptures. In this chapter the emphasis will be on the need to meditate on God's Word.

But what does meditate mean? The dictionary defines it as thinking deeply and continuously, reflecting, pondering, musing. Because meditation is often associated with Eastern religions in our society, Christians have a tendency to categorize it as the exclusive domain of skinny, bearded old men, sitting cross-legged in caves or on nails. But that's not really fair!

I'm sure you've heard of the three hermits who were so disillusioned with society and its inability to love that they decided to dedicate themselves to a life of isolation. Their rule was that none could speak except once in every five years, and then only one would be allowed to give his thought. He would be limited to single sentence.

At the end of the initial period the first of the trio was ready to share the special insight he had gained. Suddenly a great bird swooped overhead. Caught up in the excitement of the moment, he involuntarily blurted out, "My, look at that glorious eagle!" Unfortunately, his sentence was thus used up.

Five years later, the second hermit had his chance. Obviously he had been waiting a long time to say, "It wasn't an eagle. It was a hawk!" And I'm told another five years passed before the third finally stated angrily, "If you two are going to argue all the time, I'm leaving."

Putting these somewhat foolish thoughts behind us, we need to understand that meditation is a biblical concept. A few lines from Psalm 119 read, "Oh, how I love thy law! It is my meditation all the day (v. 97). . . . I revere thy commandments, which I love, and I will meditate on thy statutes (v. 48). . . . Make me understand the way of thy precepts, and I will meditate on thy wondrous works" (v. 27). The word *meditate* appears twice more in the psalm.

Following the death of Moses, God said to Joshua, "This book of the law shall not depart out of your mouth, but you shall meditate on it day and night, that you may be careful to do according to all that is written in it; for then you shall make your way prosperous, and then you shall have good success" (Josh. 1:8).

The same thought of prosperity and success resulting from meditating on God's Word is captured in Psalm 1, my text for this chapter:

> Blessed is the man who walks not in the counsel of the wicked, nor stands in the way of sinners, nor sits in the seat of scoffers; but his delight is in the law of the Lord, and on his law he meditates day and night. He is like a tree planted by streams of water, that

yields its fruit in its season, and its leaf does not wither. In all that he does, he prospers.

The wicked are not so, but are like chaff which the wind drives away. Therefore the wicked will not stand in the judgment, nor sinners in the congregation of the righteous; for the Lord knows the way of the righteous, but the way of the wicked will perish.

Let me see if I can plant a new picture of this old word, *meditation*, in your mind and bring it alive for you. Pretend that someone very important offers to share the secret of his success. You are welcome whenever you want to meet with him, even if it is at a moment's notice. But by his insistence, the visits are to be structured in a peculiar fashion.

The first half of the time this magnate or renowned artist will give you advice. Then he will stop and ask that you repeat the gist of what he has said. Once satisfied that you understand, he insists that the remaining minutes are spent quietly in his presence while you think how his words apply to your life and whether or not you will obey them. All the meetings are to follow this pattern.

Meditation is exactly this. When I talk of meditating on the Bible, I'm not suggesting that you begin searching for some mystical experience. I'm saying that God has chosen to reveal himself, among other ways, through his Word. To read a chapter here and a few verses there, hit and miss, is not adequate. You need to meditate, to read carefully and then think over the passage to make sure you understood. Finally, when still in his presence, you are to reflect on the meaning of these thoughts from

God and what possible changes need to be made in your life.

Regular meditation will inject into your spiritual bloodstream great amounts of maturity, and you will become a righteous and stable human being. That's the thrust of the passages we examined earlier. In a sentence Psalm 1 is saying: *the practice of meditation on God's Word produces stability.* Remember the psalm? The one who meditates is like a tree that yields its fruit in its season. Its leaf does not wither because it is planted by streams of water. Such a one prospers in all that he does.

I know it's hard to retain such thoughts even though they sound good, so I've incorporated them into another prayer. Last chapter's prayer was to be used before opening the Bible. This one is for immediately after having read it. With a sense of wonder, you come to the Word and feed on it. Afterwards, speak to God the following:

Father, I count it a great privilege to have just read from your eternal Word. To make sure I haven't missed anything important, I want to review the material I covered.

If I find my memory to be faulty, I'd like to scan the section again or read it through a second time. Before considering how these words apply to my life, I want to make sure I've received what you're communicating as accurately as possible.

Then take a moment to review what you've read. Having done this, continue with the prayer.

Now with a good understanding of the actual content of

this passage, I invite the Holy Spirit to apply this Word from you to my life. I intend to afford you whatever quiet time you need to reveal to me the bearing these chapters have on my life. Are my actions consistent with what I read? Is further work needed to bring my life into conformity with your divine standard? What old lessons might I have forgotten?

Again, pause and reflect on how your life compares to what you've read and the specific actions you need to take. Then continue.

I thank you for sharing with me in this time of reflection. Be assured that my intention is to live in accord with your desires. Because I believe the practice of meditation on God's Word produces stability, I would like to arrange to meet again around the sacred Scriptures on ___________. (Make plans regarding the date, time, and place for your next session in God's Word.)

Amen.

Fit a copy of this prayer into the front of your Bible. Refer to it whenever you spend time in God's Word. It can change you from a reader to a meditator, from someone with unreal expectations to a stable believer who is maturing beautifully in faith. The key, however, is to advance beyond the mere reading of the text.

A chorus my mother wrote years ago captures this reflective attitude that is so important:

Search the Scriptures daily,
You will find a wealth untold
Within the pages of God's Word,
More precious far than gold.

Take time to read the Bible,
'Tis God's message sent to you.
But as you search the Scriptures,
Let the Scriptures search you, too.

3

MASTERING

"If only I had begun earlier developing my skills, I actually think I could have . . ."

"If only I had continued in school, I could . . ."

"If only I had practiced more diligently, I . . ."

"If only I had worked harder . . ."

So many people say these words. "For of all sad words of tongue or pen," writes Whittier, "the saddest are these: it might have been."

Though the Bible is readily available to us in this day of more leisure time, only a small percentage of believers spend the time in God's Word they feel they should. Looking back over the past twelve months, most Christians can't really say they know more about God's book now than they did a year ago.

Why is this? Is it a lack of desire? I don't think so. Most believers I know sincerely want to understand the Scriptures. Maybe people are just not dedicated anymore? I don't judge that to be the difficulty either.

I personally think Christians fail to meditate on the Bible regularly because they aren't captured by a vision of what consistent study of Scripture can mean in their individual lives. Few people work just to work or study for the sake of studying or exercise merely to exercise. Behind each activity there is a goal: earning money, needing a degree in order to enter a certain profession, keeping physically fit. Could it be that God's people have lost sight of the vital reasons for meeting with him around his Word? When that happens, the discipline of Bible study has a tendency to become tedious.

Apart from a certain ingrained sense of obligation, what motivates you to get into God's Word?

Pretend you want to become a secretary to a top level executive and you go to a school that has a reputation for having trained many who hold the highest positions available in that field. The person who interviews you affirms your desire and points out skills he notices that will stand you in good stead.

"But the big problem I see," he continues, "is your present lack of ability at the typewriter. Your speed of only forty words a minute is a decided drawback and will cause you considerable embarrassment when applying for a job. Typing, you must understand, is an essential skill to the kind of work you want. Therefore, you will need to discipline yourself to improve it. Otherwise, the jobs you talk of landing are all fantasies."

The classes begin, plus hours of practice at home. As time goes on, the training gets tiresome. "How could this fool machine have the audacity to keep printing *C*'s when I'm positive I'm striking *D*'s? (mumble, grumble)

Is this really worth it?"

"Keep in mind where you're headed," responds your instructor, "and you'll be all right. It's only when you lose the vision of where you want to be some day that these hours of finger pounding no longer have meaning."

Or perhaps you just moved here from another country and you're six foot eleven. For some reason you want to try out for the school basketball team.

"I want to be a star someday!" you say to the coach.

"Well," he responds, trying to suppress his delight. "Maybe I could open a place for you in my line-up. Let me see you shoot a couple." And he tosses you a ball.

Being new to the sport you take it and aim toward the hoop. Unfortunately too much oomph wings the ball over the backboard and it lands in the drinking fountain. Several more attempts prove equally abortive. You notice the former gleam in the coach's eye fading.

"Look, what's-your-name. The object of this game is to get the ball through that little ring up there. If you can't do that, it doesn't matter if you're King Kong. Tomorrow you're going to get busy learning how to shoot. It's not going to be easy, buddy. But if you don't get started soon, the people will laugh you right off the court."

Thus begins weeks and weeks of sweat. "If you can't score," the coach keeps yelling, "a tall, skinny guy like you might as well rent himself out to the library as a bookmark!" Is it worth it? It depends on where your vision is set!

Or say you have come to know the excitement of experiencing the Lord firsthand through his Son, Jesus Christ. Now in your imagination you stand before the very God of the universe and say, "Father, more than anything else, I want to live for you. Nothing would please me more than to be always available as your servant, wherever and whenever desired."

God responds, "Thank you. I do affirm the spiritual gifts you're developing. But a basic skill needed by all key people who represent me is a good grasp of my Holy Word, both in understanding it and making it part and parcel of your life. To fall short in this area results in a lack of confidence, maturity, and spiritual assurance.

"I know it's work. But if you value my assessment at all, you'll put in the time—because you can't separate this basic ingredient from your dream of serving me well. The two always go together: studying the Word and being a first-rate disciple, an accomplished servant, an approved workman."

Listen to these words from Paul to Timothy, "Do your best to present yourself to God as one approved, a workman who has no need to be ashamed, rightly handling the word of truth" (2 Tim. 2:15).

Let me put it this way: *Approved workmen are master handlers of God's Word.*

I'm assuming you hold a dream of some day becoming all the Lord wants you to be. If not, what I have to share won't capture you. But for those who nod assent, who agree, who say "You're right, that's where I am" it's highly unlikely the dream will come true unless you allow the seed of mastering God's Word to be planted deeply within your being.

This is not an unreal challenge. In the next three to five years you have time available to become proficient at a good number of things. You can know a great deal more about a given series on television or cross-country skiing or Beethoven's music or redecorating houses or traveling—none of which is inherently good or bad in itself. But you also have the distinct possibility of mastering specific portions of Scripture. In that same time span you could tuck a good number of books of the Bible under your spiritual belt.

Would you really like to know what Colossians is about, and how its teaching affects the way you live? You could. You can also become proficient at Daniel, Luke, or Proverbs. Maybe a good friend would like to study with you, or your spouse or a son or daughter.

"David, I'm too old," you say. "I've hardly enough time left to even get started."

Maybe you're right if you think of what I'm saying only in terms of yourself. But I see outstanding Christians as the product of generations of believers. I know the Bible better than my parents do, but I also owe my start to them. I expect my four children will have every opportunity to surpass me in the way they handle this incredible book.

Even if it is late in life, you still have time to pass on to some who follow you a lasting memory of a person who valued the Scriptures. And don't forget the disicipline will be of benefit to you as well, even if you don't cover the whole book.

That's why I've written one final prayer to go along with those to help you marvel and meditate and, now, to master. Following your time of meditation, I suggest you talk to God as follows:

Father,

Before finishing this time of concentrating on your thoughts regarding the way I should live, I want to remind myself of where such sessions fit into my life.

My greatest desire is to bring honor to your son, Jesus Christ. In fact, nothing would please me more than to some day hear, "Well done, thou good and faithful servant."

I know the discipline of becoming skilled in the understanding and applying of your sacred Scriptures is basic to reaching that goal. Convinced that approved workmen are master handlers of your Word, I want to become more and more proficient.

That's why I make such times together a priority. My vision is to be a person of the Word. This is how I want others to remember me. This is the heritage I wish to pass on to those closest to me. Therefore, as the weeks and months go by I will consistently master one book of the Bible after another. Each year that passes should find me closer to my goal.

Finally, because of the effect your truth always has on my life, I am looking forward to being a markedly better person because I have invested this time. Thank you for listening as I've reminded myself of these thoughts.

Amen.

This prayer is not just a gimmick. It will work! Keep it in the front of your Bible and use it along with the other two every time you interact with God's Word. Marvel over, meditate on, and master the Scripture. Change the "if only I hads" into "I dids." Enjoy your well-won sense of excitement and progress.

4

LOST AND FOUND

Two Old Testament stories that are not frequently expounded teach a similar lesson. The first takes place in Jerusalem under young King Josiah. He was only eight years old when he came to the throne after the assassination of Amon, his evil father. At this time Israel, the northern kingdom, already had fallen to Assyria and for almost fifty years the rulers and people of southern Judah had lived far below God's expectations.

Second Chronicles 34 reads:

> In the eighth year of his reign, while he was yet young [sixteen], he began to seek after *and* yearn for the God of David his father [forefather]; and in the twelfth year he began to purge Judah and Jerusalem of the high places, the Asherim, and the carved and molten images (v. 3) . . . . In the eighteenth year of Josiah's reign . . . he (sent men) to repair the house of

the Lord his God" (v 8). In the process "Hilkiah the priest found the book of the law of the Lord given by Moses" (The Amplified Bible,v. 14).

My personal feeling is that this discovery was not just a matter of chance. God always sees to it that his Word is found when people begin to return to him.

In that era of ancient Israel, it was time for God to bring to light the beauty of his book. "When King Josiah had heard the words of the law, he rent his clothes, . . . because our fathers have not kept the word of the Lord, to do according to all that is written in this book (vv. 19-21).

But God replied, "Because your heart was tender *and* penitent and you humbled yourself before God, . . . and rent your clothes and wept before me, I have heard you" (The Amplified Bible) (v. 27).

A similar account is found in Nehemiah. At this moment in history, about a century and a half after the first incident, God had allowed the southern kingdom of Judah to be conquered because of her continued wickedness. This time it is the Babylonians who do the honors, and they take vast numbers of Jewish people into exile.

Once again, the record is one of Judah's failure to live up to God's expectations. In time Persia conquered Babylon, and under divine providence the new rulers permitted certain Hebrews to return to their native land.

One such delegation is formed under Nehemiah, who has been cupbearer for the Persian king. Deeply burdened for his people and his homeland, the account opens with his touching prayer.

> O Lord God of Heaven, . . . let thy ear be attentive, and thy eyes open, to hear the prayer of thy servant which I now pray before thee day and night. . . . Yea, I and my father's house have sinned. We have acted very corruptly against thee, and have not kept the commandments, the statutes, and the ordinances which thou didst command thy servant Moses, . . . saying, "If you are unfaithful, I will scatter you among the peoples; but if you return to me and keep my commandments and do them, though your dispersed be under farthest skies, I will gather them thence and bring them to the place which I have chosen, to make my name dwell there" (Neh. 1:5-9).

Nehemiah's prayer was answered, and soon he was leading a delegation of 50,000 of his people back across 900 miles of caravan trails to Jerusalem where his party, under great duress, rebuilt the walls of the city.

Having made great effort to honor the Lord,

> All the people gathered as one man into the square before the Water Gate; and they told Ezra the scribe to bring the book of the law of Moses which the LORD had given to Israel. And Ezra the priest brought the law before the assembly, . . . and he read it . . . from early morning until midday . . . , and the ears of all the people were attentive to the book of the law (Neh. 8:1-3).

So, once again, and this time not possibly by accident but by the deliberate request of people who desired to honor God in their lives, the sacred writings became very important. When the Word was read, there was an emotional response. Tears came to the people's eyes.

> And Nehemiah, who was the governor, and Ezra the priest and scribe, and the Levites who taught the people said to all the people, "This day is holy to our LORD your God; do not mourn or weep." For all the people wept when they heard the words of the law. Then he said to them, "Go your way, eat the fat and drink sweet wine . . . , for this day is holy to our Lord; and do not be grieved, for the joy of the Lord is your strength." So the Levites stilled all the people and they went their way to eat and drink . . . and to make great rejoicing, because they had understood the words that were declared to them (Neh. 8:9-12).

Here then are two accounts of the Lord's people beginning to seek him and to live obediently. In each case it isn't very long before God's Word is playing a central role in transforming their lives. When any individual or group of people set their hearts on knowing God, it is natural that the Scriptures will quickly begin to play a key role in the fulfilling of such desires. In other words: *Those desiring to honor God soon rediscover the beauty of Scripture.*

Perhaps you're someone who feels you've not lived up to what God expected, but in the last month you've made new efforts to honor him and his claims on your life. It may not seem like much to someone else, but to you it has been a great step of faith to start giving some of your money to the Lord's work, or to begin looking for a church home again even though you were terribly hurt where you last attended.

You are to be commended for the way you made right that wrong you committed so long ago. Until the matter was rectified, you couldn't have made any significant spiritual progress. Yet, you did it even though it was hard. Well, I think it's great.

And you, sir, after fighting against it for so long, are now going to be baptized. Good for you!

Before long, if you are really serious about knowing God, there will come an overpowering awareness that you need to give special attention to the Bible. It may be unexpectedly as in Josiah's day. Or it may come about in a very matter-of-fact fashion, as to Nehemiah. But the conviction will come that God's Word is essential in your life.

"Oh, I wish you hadn't said that," I hear someone react. "Ever since I was little the necessity of studying the Scriptures has been crammed down my throat. No news could be worse than what you've just said, David."

Don't panic! If the appetite doesn't come, I won't force-feed you. I'm only saying that when people really want to know God, some supernatural lever inside them begins to pressure them toward the Word.

Think about those people who are serious about mastering a musical instrument. They finally accept the fact that practice is a must.

If people are excited about how they will look and feel after losing thirty pounds, they won't fight a change in eating habits. If one sincerely wants to improve a bad marriage, he will willingly examine such basics as commitment and communication. To refuse to be open to such realities is to forfeit the dream.

So it is with the lofty ambition of knowing God intimately. This goal won't be accomplished without time spent in his Word. To believe otherwise is to be unrealistic.

So I urge you—refuse to allow past negative feelings to keep you from the worthy desire of drawing close to the Lord. Since there is progress, and so far you've not been disappointed, you might even discover the Scriptures to be beautiful at this time in your life. Instead of indifference, now there are tears. Passages that seemed irrelevant now boom and thunder. Start, and you wonder why newspapers and magazines and television have suddenly become so dull in comparison.

"David, I have trouble getting started," you say. "Where do I begin reading? I guess none of it sounds interesting to me anymore."

Let me give you five suggestions, and as you examine these, keep my main idea in the back of your mind: Those who desire to honor God soon rediscover the beauty of Scripture.

Genesis 37-50 records the story of Joseph. Not only is this an easy and interesting narrative, it's good material for reflection and meditation. If you cry while reading, know that you're normal.

A similar section that's a little shorter would be Daniel 1-6.

If you're more ambitious, tackle the books of First and Second Samuel. All told, there are fifty-five chapters of Scripture that are very helpful, especially if you've lately felt misunderstood and trespassed against.

Finally, let me propose two New Testament books.

The Gospel of Luke is an early biography of Christ through the eyes of a medical doctor. I suggest Luke because if you like his style, it's natural to read his sequel, the Book of Acts.

And finally, a short letter from John, the man who was closest to Christ during his earthly pilgrimage. Later in life John wrote an epistle or letter that takes up only four pages in the average-size Bible and appears under the title of First John. I think you'll find that the advice he gives is timeless.

If you like what he says, read the next two brief letters from his pen, Second and Third John, plus his eyewitness account of Jesus' life. You'll find this very different in style from Luke's. John also wrote the final book of the Bible, Revelation.

Well, that should start you off, and maybe that's the biggest part of the battle.

May it be with you as it was with the Israelites after their fresh encounter with the Word: "The people went their way . . . rejoicing, because they understood the words [of the Lord] that were declared to them."

5

KNOWING THE LANGUAGE

In order to spend more time with my children and also to insure that I'm a little more rounded culturally, I've been participating in a pottery class with my nine-year-old son, Joel. I've thoroughly enjoyed myself.

Along with becoming familiar with the wheel and the clay, we've had to learn some pottery language. To me, *slip* had always been what happened to some unfortunate soul on ice or something my wife wore. But now I've learned it's also the water/clay mixture that's used as a lubricant when shaping the spinning clay. *Grog* isn't served to drink; it is part of the recipe that makes the clay. And *throw* is not what you angrily do with pieces you don't like, but the process of lifting the walls of a cup or pitcher or bowl.

For a while it seemed all I did was ask, "Now, what did you just say?" or answer Joel's "What's that word mean, daddy?" I remember thinking, *A new apprentice* almost needs a sheet with basic definitions before he takes up this craft.

Then it hit me. I wonder what it's like for new Christians when they hear certain "in" words. How could they know what a spiritual gift is? Or would they not likely give a wrong shade of meaning to the word *prophet* and see him only as someone who predicts the future?

I began to make a list of possible problem words for new believers.

To my surprise, the list quickly became too long. In an effort of cut back, I decided to keep only words ending in *i-o-n*. There were still too many. *Let's see,* I thought, *making it t-i-o-n-ending words would eliminate problems,* like *intercession,* and what it means to *commission* someone. *Confession* and *conversion* were dropped. This also freed me from having to explain *circumcision* (another "Daddy, what's that mean?" word).

Alas, the list was still too lengthy. So I chose to add an *a* to my endings. The words I'll explain must now end in *a-t-i-o-n.* That should help, I figured. So, *absolution, substitution, petition, persecution, redemption* and *adoption* went by the wayside.

Reduced considerably, my list of difficult words to explain to a newcomer was still longer than desired. Instead of just one more letter, I added two. I'll only explain words that end in *i-c-a-t-i-o-n.* Now I'll not have to deal with such terms as *regeneration, expiation, dispensation, tribulation, proclamation, invitation, separation of the believer, manifestation of the spirit, meditation* on the Scriptures, *exhortation, consecration, interpretation,* or *libation.* The *abomination* of *desolation* puts two confusers off the list together. Is that all? No. There's *reconciliation, visitation, indignation,* and *vexation—creation*—plus the realization this explanation idea with which I began can bring frustration to the man who attempts to solve this problem in one fell swoop!

My list still included *supplication, vindication, justification, glorification,* and one more.

But I think my point's been made. The "in" talk of the church is possibly the most difficult of all to learn. And yet, in order to become strong in the Christian walk, understanding is very important.

I suppose I could have limped on in this pottery class, attempting to figure out the definitions of the terms my instructor uses. But I've opted from the beginning to ask for help when necessary. Fortunately, this teacher has proven to be very cooperative. Even so, I think he's so used to saying cones and kilns and pitters and shaping-ribs that he can hardly keep from using these words. So I figure the major responsibility of closing this communication gap has to rest with young Joel and his dad. We're learning to ask, "What does that word mean?"

I'm convinced that knowing this language enhances the work of the potter. What is also true in my mind is that *knowing the language enhances the skills of the believer.*

In that context, I'm reminded of the account in Acts 8 where the angel talks to Philip:

"Go toward the south to the road that goes down from Jerusalem to Gaza. . . . And he rose and went. And behold, an Ethiopian, a eunuch, a minister of

Candace the queen of the Ethiopians, in charge of all her treasure, had come to Jerusalem to worship and was returning; seated in his chariot, he was reading the prophet Isaiah. And the Spirit said to Philip, "Go up and join this chariot." So Philip ran to him and . . . asked, "Do you understand what you are reading?" And he said, "How can I, unless someone guides me?" (vv. 26-31).

There's a happy ending to this story, because understanding came where before there had been confusion.

There is only one word left on my list to explain to new believers. Have you figured out what it is? That's right: *sanctification.* It appears frequently throughout the Bible and preachers use it quite often. But who knows what it means? There's an old saying that many expositors unconsciously emulate: "I know you think you understand what I said, but just be aware that what you thought you heard me say is not really what I meant."

For practice then, let's explore this one word. To sanctify something is to set it apart as holy. An easy way to remember this is to think of a sanctuary, which is a place set apart for God's use. The word *saint* comes from the same root and means "a sanctified one," or a person belonging to God.

In the Old Testament, you remember, the Levites were the tribe separated from the others for God's service. In similar fashion, the Sabbath was one day in seven that belonged exclusively to the Lord. For that matter, Israel, unique among the nations, was also sanctified. This word, one of the most important in the entire Bible, has to do with being set apart for the Lord.

In the New Testament, this work of being set apart unto the Lord is begun in each true believer by the Holy Spirit. When a person first becomes a Christian, the Spirit of God literally comes to indwell that individual. The Apostle Paul states that our bodies are temples, dwelling places, of the Lord.

But in another sense, the hallowing process (sanctification) has only begun, and now it's up to you to honor the Spirit's every desire in your life. As you do so, or as you obey the promptings of the Spirit, the result is sanctification, or continuing to be set apart for God's special use.

Paul writes in Romans 6:22, "Now that you have been set free from sin, which is another way of saying "set, apart unto God," the return you get is sanctification."

So, then, here's a beautiful word. In the New Testament we are all regarded as believer-priests, not just one tribe out of twelve. In that unique role, it's very important not to follow the waywardness of our Old Testament counterparts. Sanctification is a great blessing that dare not be abused. Understand?

"Sanctification, yes," you say, "now that you've explained it. But many of the other words you mentioned are still confusing."

Which is why I'll give you two simple suggestions. One, keep a sheet of paper in your Bible, and whenever you're not sure you understand a word, write it down. Then as you have time, find out what it means.

This leads me to suggestion number two. A good investment for a believer serious about his or her faith is a Bible dictionary or encyclopedia. Available at any

Christian bookstore or by mail from several major Christian publishers, the investment is well worth the cost.

And before long, who knows. I'll be making better pots along with my son Joel, and you'll be growing stronger as a believer. And we'll all be exultant—ah, enraptured (I wonder what that means?)—ah, transported . . .

6

A SURE WORD

"Now this weapon's a little tough to master at first, gentlemen. But once you get the hang of it, you'll know you have one phenomenal tool of destruction in your hands. What do you say? Do you want to learn how to fire this thing or not?"

"Yeah," some recruits impressed with the demonstration rounds, may say. But those who take the offer most seriously are soldiers who know what it's like to be on the front lines. With that experience, they know only too well the value of a good instrument of warfare.

Those of you who understand spiritual warfare from firsthand experience will be delighted to know about a highly effective weapon. A little investment of time with it will do wonders for you—both offensively and defensively. Christ was a master of this war tool. Are you interested?

The other night my children and I watched an old

Walt Disney film called *The Jungle Book*. Maybe you've seen it. It's an extremely free adaptation in cartoon form of Rudyard Kipling's original story. One of the characters is Kaa, the snake. He's a huge rock python who hypnotizes his victims with his psychedelic eyes. I know snakes don't possess hypnotic powers, but this one does.

Swaying back and forth he sings a song that causes his victims' pupils to spin until they're totally in his power. My younger sons bought the record, and the words this snake sings are fresh in my mind: "Trust in me. Trust in me. Shut your eyes, and trust in me. You can sleep, safe and sound, knowing I am around. Slip into silent slumber, sail on a silver mist. Slowly and surely your senses will cease to resist . . ."

Well, there's not a kid who doesn't know this python is a liar. The corporate body language of every child watching said, "Don't trust him! Stay away! Avoid looking at his eyes little man cub! Run!"

I wish Christians would feel as strongly regarding the advances of the tempter in their everyday life. "Trust in me," he says. "Trust in me. Oh, my coils, will feel fine. I'm your friend, I know how, to give you, what is mine."

There is no logical reason for you to fall for such phony lines. But somehow, when Satan dangles his bait and begins to wave it back and forth, it seems to be the only thing in the world that matters.

Shere Khan is the big tiger in *The Jungle Book*. While they talk together the reptile begins weaving his spell in self-defense, "Trust in me, Tiger, trust in me," and his eyes start their magic.

Almost immediately—thunk!—a great orange and

black paw is on the head of the serpent. A long, sharp nail is placed squarely on the snake's nose. "I don't have any time for that foolishness," says the tiger's deep voice.

"Wow! That's something," you say along with all the children. "I want to be like that tiger!" Then pay attention, for what I have to share will help make that dream come true.

We're talking about the availability of a very effective instrument of spiritual warfare. Frequently Jesus said, "I don't have time for that foolishness," and the enemy, totally humiliated, left him.

This same technique has often been employed by spiritual heros for mounting offensives. What is it? Memorization of the Scriptures.

"Oh, mister, you're silly," you say. "That's kid stuff, primary department. I've got bad memories of all that work, and me forgetting my verses in front of all the parents. Memorize Scripture? Not on your life. Besides, I'm too old."

Okay, however you want it. Though it's funny how hard you work in other areas to prove you're not aging. I'll continue for the sake of those who want help in spiritual warfare but are realistic enough to know that some problems of life aren't solved through wishing. Are you a person who can appreciate the value of a proven weapon?

In a sentence, what I'm saying is this: *Memorizing Scripture is extremely helpful for spiritual warfare.* "I have laid up thy Word in my heart," wrote the psalmist (119:11), "that I might not sin against thee."

I have learned that not only does Bible memorization

ingrain truths in my mind and heart, it really isn't hard if two simple rules are followed. One, carefully choose the material you want to memorize. Obviously, you're no longer motivated to learn fifty unrelated verses and the references in order to go to camp free. That incentive is gone. Most of you are adults now. You don't need an arbitrary list. Rather, commit verses to memory that are relevant to your own situation.

If you have trouble telling the truth, don't memorize Psalm 23. Find some Scripture that speaks about lying, learn it by heart. Then the next time you're tempted to exaggerate grab onto God's Word.

Psalm 34:12, 13 would be good: "What man is there who desires life, and covets many days, that you may enjoy good? Keep your tongue from evil, and your lips from speaking deceit."

Or Proverbs 25:18: "A man who bears false witness against his neighbor is like a war club, or a sword, or a sharp arrow." Half the fun is finding what you are looking for. Then complete the process by making it your own.

Right now I'm working on verses that help me understand the greatness of God when I pray. When I'm busy, it's hard to quickly enter into the privilege of speaking personally to the very God of the universe. Therefore I'm working on Isaiah 6:

> In the year that King Uzziah died I saw the Lord sitting upon a throne, high and lifted up; and his train filled the temple. Above him stood the seraphim; each had six wings: with two he covered his face, and with two he covered his feet, and with two he flew. And

one called to another and said: "Holy, holy, holy is the Lord of hosts; the whole earth is full of his glory." And the foundations of the thresholds shook at the voice of him who called, and the house was filled with smoke (vv. 1-4).

Being able to recall a passage like this, along with others I have in mind, help me be conscious of the one to whom I speak when I pray. And, of course, prayer is also a big part of spiritual warfare.

Carefully choose the material you want to memorize. Make sure the portion you pick relates directly to the needs you feel, whether that be sharing your faith, being concerned for the poor, overcoming lust, or whatever.

Once the passage has been chosen, my second rule is to set aside an initial half hour for hard work. This is the key. I repeat: set aside a half hour for memorizing, say next Saturday afternoon, or Tuesday night, or early Friday morning. A half hour isn't that long; it's only the time of the average television program.

Keep the appointment and work on making the verse or verses you chose your own. Once the initial half hour has been achieved, completing the job by reviewing is rather easy. I have just finished learning the first ten verses of Ephesians 2. A half hour on a Sunday afternoon got me off to a great start.

"Trust in me . . . trust in me . . ." Do you hear the music in the background? Are you coming under the influence of that serpent, our great enemy? Fire the weapon. Quote your memorized Scripture. Say with Christ, "Be quiet! There's no time for that foolishness!"

7

IT'S ALL TRUE

I'd like to share just one remembrance of a trip I made to Israel with my wife and oldest son, Randy. I promise not to refer to the Holy Land again in this book. I know sometimes people who make that trip are almost as hard to get rid of as the omnipresent peddlers of beads you run into while there.

One thing I hadn't anticipated before visiting Israel was an awareness of the profound influence of the Romans on this tiny land. Though thirteen hundred years have passed, somehow the Roman presence is still felt. The ancient ghostly landlord remains. Part of this is due to the fact that the Romans were master builders. Whether it's the name of a city like Tiberias on the Sea of Galilee or an ancient theatre overlooking the Mediterranean in Caesarea or the wailing wall in Jerusalem, one has to admit that imperial momentos are still very much there.

I believe the name most often referred to by our tour guide was that of Herod the Great. I had rightly pegged him as the ruler who was alarmed by the visit of the wise men from the East as recorded in Matthew two. Not long before he died he ordered the slaughter of all male children in Bethlehem two years old or under to be sure no new Jewish king would threaten his crown.

But I hadn't realized what a phenomenal builder this Herod was until I went to Masada. This incredible fortress on a stark, rocky cliff in the wilderness overlooking the Dead Sea is now ascended by tourists in a cable car. Any who desire can also hike the so-called snake path that winds its tortuous way up the side of the mountain. In fact, as we were leaving the cable car and preparing to climb the last eighty or so steps, two sweaty young men were just finishing the hour and a half ascent on foot.

One, obviously exhausted but with his sense of humor intact, said to his companion, "You know, I bet when we finally get to the top, there'll be some enterprising fellow there smiling and waiting to sell us a string of beads!" Anyway, Herod's Masada, with its huge water cisterns and steam baths and three-level winter palace, to say nothing of its extensive fortifications, remains an engineering wonder.

Herod's crowning achievement was to be created in Jerusalem itself. Having built his new palace and citadel with towers at the highest point of the upper city, he controlled a view for miles around. Near the old temple, which dated to the time of Zerubbabel, he constructed the massive fortress Antonio (named after Mark Antony). His beautified city was also endowed with a theater, a hippodrome or track for chariot races, a gymnasium, and public baths.

The "most glorious of all his actions," wrote Josephus in his *Antiquities of the Jews,* was the construction of a new temple and "this was to be sufficient for an everlasting memorial of him." Preparation alone took two years.

A labor force of some ten-thousand workmen was assembled, including a thousand priests trained as masons and carpenters to do the work inside the sanctuary where laymen were forbidden. A thousand carts and wagons were acquired to transport the huge quantities of stone and other building materials. The actual construction was started in 20 B.C., and the temple structure itself was erected in eighteen months. But the completion of the great complex of buildings, courtyards, and adornment took forty-six years in all. It was not completed until a generation after Herod's death.

On our first day of visiting, the three Mains family members stood at the wailing, or western, wall and were amazed at not only its size but the immensity of the stones from the Roman New Testament period. One of them visible today is forty feet long. Another stone twenty-four by six feet has an estimated weight of over one hundred tons!

This retaining wall, which is not a part of the temple itself, stands against the large elevated land mass on which the temple was erected.

As early as the third and fourth centuries A.D., there were rabbis who referred to this wall as being especially sacred, just because it was close to the Holy of Holies of the demolished temple where the divine presence was thought to linger.

Overwhelmed by the size of these projects, I realized how soldiers quartered at the fortress Antonia kept a continual vigil over the entire temple area. The courage Christ must have displayed caught me offguard. Not only did he publicly preach there, but twice he cleared the court area of money changers. And suddenly my mind also pictured his triumphal entry into the city at Passover to the shouts of the people's hosannas: "Save, we pray! Now!" It gave me a chill. Christ allowed himself to be swept into inevitable conflict and death.

Still attempting to sort out the myriad impressions coming to me, we later visited the Holy Land Hotel, where a magnificient outdoor model of Jerusalem during the time of Christ has been built to scale by a professor from the Hebrew University. The section of the western wall that still stands has been marked so the viewer can put everything into place. Once again one wonders, how in the face of Rome's great strength Christ had the fortitude to walk within those city walls with his little band of twelve, preaching an alternative Kingdom?

Standing on the eastern side of the model city (which I estimated to be about fifty yards across), I looked directly at the impressive model temple on the elevated mount. How solid and impregnable it all appeared. How massive the wall! How strong its fortifications! How beautiful and elaborate!

Then of a sudden, some incredible words came to my mind from Luke 21. Christ was teaching in those last days before his death. "As for these things which you see, the days will come when there shall not be left here one stone upon another that will not be thrown down" (v. 6).

How could he have known? No one in his right mind would have predicted such a thing! This long-range building project had just been completed the year after Christ began his public ministry. There was no way to respond to such an outlandish prophecy except to smile and nod a polite "maybe so."

Yet only three decades passed before the prediction was precisely fulfilled. On the same day of the year in which, more than six centuries earlier, Nebuchadnezzar's Babylonian soldiers had destroyed the first temple and sacked Jerusalem, the Romans under Titus repeated the act in 70 A. D.

In the words of the historian Josephus, "The flames of fire were so violent and impetuous that the mountain on which the temple stood resembled one large body of fire, even from its foundations."

Through the pall of smoke the Roman soldiers ran amuck, looting and killing. Titus and his entourage managed to enter the sanctuary before it was destroyed and carry off some of the vessels and furnishings that later reached Rome. On orders from Titus the city was then razed except for the three towers of the citadel and the city wall on the west. These were left as protection for the tenth legion posted as a garrison. The temple area was leveled stone by stone. Those inhabitants who were not butchered were hauled off to be thrown to wild animals in the arenas of Caesarea, Antioch, or Rome— or were sold as slaves.

As I stood there it was all so chilling to me. I could feel

my body actually reacting to the wonder of the experience! There was no question about it, Jesus was
unique! *The fulfillment of Christ's prophecies encourages confidence in all he said.*

Once again my trust in God's Word was suddenly
affirmed. What has been shared with us in the Bible is
indeed the very truth of the universe. I can study it with
a sense of assurance. There is no volume like the sacred
Scriptures.

Maybe you would like to read just a little more from
Christ's famous Olivet discourse beyond what I've
quoted so far.

They will fall by the edge of the sword, and be led
captive among all nations; and Jerusalem will be
trodden down by the Gentiles, until the times of the
Gentiles are fulfilled.

And there will be signs in sun and moon and stars,
and upon the earth distress of nations in perplexity at
the roaring of the sea and the waves, men fainting
with fear and with foreboding of what is coming on the
world; for the powers of the heavens will be shaken.
And then they will see the Son of man coming in a
cloud with power and great glory. Now when these
things begin to take place, look up and raise your
heads, because your redemption is drawing near.
(Luke 21:25-28).

But take heed to yourselves lest your hearts be
weighed down with dissipation and drunkenness and
cares of this life, and that day come upon you
suddenly like a snare; for it will come upon all who
dwell upon the face of the whole earth. But watch at

all times, praying that you may have strength to escape all these things that will take place, and to stand before the Son of man (vv. 34-36).

I believe what is written. The partial fulfillment of these words encourages confidence in the total.

8
MYSTERY

Tevya, the poor Russian dairyman in the story *Fiddler on the Roof,* finds himself in the middle of an intense argument.

"It was a horse," shouts a man on one side.

"You're right," says Tevya.

"It was a mule!" yells a representative of the others.

"You're right!" responds Tevya, now caught up in what's going on.

"Wait a minute," interjects a third party. "If *he's* right, how can *he* be right also?"

Tevya thinks briefly, and then utters his classic reply, "You're right!"

This chapter may have a little of that same flavor, because I'd like to deal with a word that comes up rather frequently in the Scriptures—namely, *mystery.*

What brought this to mind was a recent weighty discussion with my youngest son about how God wasn't born, but always has been and always will be.

"That's because he's eternal," I confidently told Jeremy. But it was easier said than explained to his satisfaction! After a while, my five year old concluded that what I was saying about God was kind of funny; and that it was true anyway, because his daddy said it was.

Frankly, that's the attitude I've adopted regarding certain doctrines I still find puzzling when I study the Bible. Sometimes they don't make total sense to me, but I accept them because they're affirmed by the word of my heavenly Father.

Take, for example, the nature of Christ. I affirm Jesus to be 100 percent divine. He's the very Son of Almighty God himself. But I also hold that he is 100 percent man as the offspring of the Virgin Mary. He experienced humanity just as we do.

"Wait a minute," you say. "If he's 100 percent divine, how can he also be 100 percent human? That's confusing!"

You're right! It is confusing but, nevertheless, true. To retreat on either aspect of Christ's nature would be to go against both Scripture and the church.

I have similar feelings during discussions about the doctrine of the Trinity. I worship one God and yet I sing in all honesty: "Holy, Holy, Holy! Lord God Almighty! All Thy works shall praise Thy name, in earth, and sky, and sea; Holy, Holy, Holy! Merciful and Mighty! God in Three Persons, blessed Trinity!" The nature of God is tripartisan, with each of the three personalities of the Godhead being distinctly different.

I even find some of this bewildering element in terms of my everyday ministry. To fulfill my responsibilities, how much should I work and how much should I pray? There's a tension in life between activism and piety. Cardinal Spellman said one should pray as though everything depended on God, and work as though all was dependent on self. That's not bad advice—until you try to follow it. When you truly pray as though everything depended on God, you don't have time to work as though everything depended on self!

Boiled down to a sentence, my thoughts could be summarized as follows: *Scripture reminds us of the mystery of our faith.*

Observe these sample verses that use the word: "That utterance may be given me in opening my mouth boldly to proclaim the mystery of the gospel" (Eph. 6:19).

"Great indeed, we confess, is the mystery of our religion" (1 Tim. 3:16).

"Deacons . . . must hold the mystery of the faith with a clear conscience" (1 Tim. 3:9).

"This is how one should regard us, as servants of Christ and stewards of the mysteries of God" (1 Cor. 4:1).

"And pray for us also, that God may open us a door for the word, to declare the mystery of Christ" (Col. 4:3).

I'm aware that the Greek word used here carries with it the idea of something previously hidden or unknown that has been revealed by God. But this word also contains the concept of God's wisdom being far more marvelous than our own. As he reveals his truth it is glorious beyond any ideas we might have conceived. Isaiah 55 comes to mind in this regard: "For my thoughts are not your thoughts, neither are your ways my ways, says the Lord. For as the heavens are higher than the earth, so are my ways higher than your ways and my thoughts than your thoughts" (vv. 8, 9).

Theologians have argued points of doctrine throughout the years, and there's great value in sharpening what one believes. But when talking about certain issues where the natural and supernatural combine, it is judicious to remember that man's intellect might not be able to understand fully what God's Word teaches. Are we not wise to remain open to this element of mystery?

Let me give an example. I believe Scripture teaches that no human can come to God unless the Almighty draws that one to himself. A passage like Romans 9 is very strong on this point:

> For he [God] says to Moses, "I will have mercy on whom I have mercy, and I will have compassion on whom I have compassion." So it depends not upon man's will or exertion, but upon God's mercy. For the scripture says to Pharaoh, "I have raised you up for the very purpose of showing my power in you, so that my name may be proclaimed in all the earth." So then he has mercy upon whomever he wills, and he hardens the heart of whomever he wills (vv. 15-18).

We can conclude from this that God chooses those who are to be his. On the other hand, I also feel we are responsible to choose God. Since salvation depends on God choosing me, why should I also feel as though my eternal destiny rested upon my choosing God? This is a baffling union of truths, and yet that flavor also marks the Bible.

Who can deny there is a consistent appeal throughout the pages of Scripture for all humanity to come to

God? "Come to me, all who labor and are heavy laden, and I will give you rest," promises Christ (Matt. 12:28). "God is not willing that any should perish but that all should come to repentance." Why such sweeping invitations if we don't really have a free choice?

In all honesty, I don't have trouble living with these complementary concepts of predestination and free will. It's just that academically it's hard to understand precisely how they fit together. At that point I resolve the issue by saying it's a part of the mystery of our faith. If that sounds like a cop-out, the stance is really no different from the conclusion I drew regarding God the three in one, or Christ being both divine and human.

People sometimes seem ashamed to admit an inability to grasp the wonder of God and how he involves himself in our world. But maybe we should be quicker to confess that it's very hard to reduce God and what he does to our theologically consistent framework. In doing so, we appear to destroy some of the mystery that the Bible itself contains.

For that matter, today we witness this exact dilemma regarding the very book that reveals the truth about himself. Is the Bible really a sacred volume? Why there's no question about that. It's 100 percent divine.

"Then it's not human, as some people think?"

I didn't say that—it's 100 percent human also.

"How can that be?" you ask.

Well, I would have said you couldn't have a person who was 100 percent human and 100 percent divine at the same time. But God sent Christ anyway. Rather than struggle to force my mind to figure how and why, I've just chosen to accept this marvelous truth about

Christ—the past, present, and future King over all.

Once that step of faith was taken, it made it easier for me to appreciate other such wonders of the Almighty. His eternal written Word, for instance, the very truth of God himself somehow distinctly marked by the various personalities of those who wrote under the inspiration of the Holy Spirit. To minimize either the supernatural or the natural elements is to damage the total. How does one explain the miracle of Scripture without resorting to a word like mystery? For me it is next to impossible.

Are there any of these issues of mystery over which the church has not fought down through the years? Usually during such divisive periods people on both sides quote verses from the Bible to support their conclusions. Could it possibly be both parties hold to a part of the truth, but still need the emphasis of the other side to have the whole truth? Though they seem to be fighting over irreconcilable differences, in reality they both affirm part of that which makes up the great mystery of the faith.

Let's take man's eternal destiny. John 10:27-29 says:

> My sheep hear my voice, and I know them, and they follow me; and I give them eternal life, and they shall never perish, and no one shall snatch them out of my hand. My Father, who has given them to me, is greater than all, and no one is able to snatch them out of the Father's hand.

How does that correlate with Hebrews 3:14, which doesn't seem to present so secure a picture? "For we share in Christ, if only we hold our first confidence firm to the end." Or with 2 Peter 2:21-22:

> For it would have been better for them never to have known the way of righteousness than after knowing it to turn back from the holy commandment delivered to them. It has happened to them according to the true proverb, The dog turns back to his own vomit, and the sow is washed only to wallow in the mire.

Do these verses represent an impasse between those who hold to eternal security and those who advocate the perservance of the saints? No, not unless one insists that humans can totally understand the supernatural, tucking in all the loose ends so no questions remain. In my thinking, there is a difference between biblical theology and man's attempt to systematize it.

I am not implying we believe in nonsense. It's just that sometimes we may take our ability to make all truth totally rational too seriously.

A flea riding on a great elephant's head as the huge beast crossed a bridge is the center of a story my dad often tells. Upon reaching the other side, a tiny voice was heard to say, "My, didn't we shake that bridge!" I wonder if that's not somewhat the presumptous way of man as he fancies himself sitting atop God's truth!

If there is nothing inexplicable in what you believe, perhaps your theology needs shaking. To be more exact, *Scripture reminds us of the mystery of our faith.*

9

BEING IN LOVE

Have you ever fancied yourself in love with a beautiful maiden or a handsome prince? If so, you will probably enjoy studying one of the short books found in the poetical section of the Old Testament: The Song of Solomon.

Defined by Webster, poetry is "the embodiment in appropriate language of beautiful or high thought— what is written being rhythmical, usually metrical, and adapted to arouse feelings and imagination." The word conveys the idea of being beyond or above history, more of an idealization. Therefore, The Song of Solomon shouldn't be forced into strict historical accuracy like the romances of Ruth or Esther.

The song itself is composed of approximately six pages of well-written lovemaking from the pen of King Solomon:

You have ravished my heart with a glance of your eyes, with one jewel of your necklace. How sweet is your love . . . better than wine, and the fragrance of your oils than any spice! Your lips distill nectar, my bride; honey and milk are under your tongue; the scent of your garments is like the scent of Lebanon (4:9-11).

Let me warn you. When you first read the book, be prepared to find it somewhat confusing, since the Scriptures don't supply information as to who is making what statement. The traditional interpretation is that Solomon is the lover throughout, and his bride is a beautiful Shulammite girl. This, however, presents some major problems with certain portions of the text.

A second approach, which relieves some of these complications, is to set up a triangle between the maiden, her true lover (a shepherd boy), and King Solomon, who views the young woman's beauty while she tends the flocks and wants to make her one of his wives. She, however, struggles against this because of her love for the shepherd.

Some passages make far more sense under this kind of an arrangement. For example, her comment to the women of the court, "Why should you look upon the Shulammite, as upon a dance before two armies?" Or her repeated pleas: "I adjure you, O daughters of Jerusalem, by the gazelles or the hinds of the field, that you stir not up nor awaken love until it please" (2:7; 3:5). Or the conclusion to the book when she says: "Solomon had a vineyard at Baal-Hamon; he let out the vineyard to keepers; each one was to bring for its fruit a thousand pieces of silver. My vineyard, my very own [in other words, my body] is for myself" (8:11-12).

If you have never read The Song of Solomon with this third person possibility, do so, and see if it helps. No interpretation solves all the problems, and the text remains a mystery under any circumstance. Maybe this is a part of its appeal.

One way or another, the book glorifies romantic love in a mature fashion, and in doing so places scriptural sanction upon it.

Several years ago I remember watching Billy Graham being interviewed on the "Tonight Show." When the conversation got around to pornography, Johnny Carson asked, "But what about The Song of Solomon? Aren't there some pretty hot parts in that, Billy?"

To an individual with any degree of social maturity, the answer has to be "No!" If one can get his "kicks" out of reading through The Song of Solomon he's maladjusted indeed! The topic of sex is not avoided in Scripture, but it's always handled in a mature manner, and such is the case with this Old Testament passage.

Many people sanction the book's position in the Bible by saying it is symbolic. In other words, the romance it portrays is a type of God's love for Israel (or in our day, Christ's love for his church). Though there's no need for such justification, there is validity in being open to this stance. God would then be represented by Solomon in the first rendition, or the shepherd lover in the second. In either case the Shulammite is Israel, or God's people. Thus the story becomes a greater picture of God offering his love to his own, either as the King or the Shepherd. The maiden responds in turn as the people of the Lord.

Because the purpose of the book is not didactic, it's difficult to draw lessons from it. Maybe to do so would be inconsistent with its very nature. Allow me then to choose a theme that will fit any of these interpretations without forcing one above the other.

A characteristic of those in love is the desire to be in one another's presence. This emphasis is obvious as one reads through the book: "Awake, O north wind, and come, O south wind! Blow upon my garden, let its fragrance be wafted abroad. Let my beloved come to his garden, and eat of its choicest fruits" (4:16).

If you were madly in love with someone but had no desire to see that person, a problem would be present. Or if the one you adored had no inclination whatsoever to be near you, something would be equally peculiar. When people who love each other are apart, it's normal to have pleasant thoughts about meeting again. In fact, one might anticipate the event regularly during the day.

People in love are preoccupied with thoughts of the other, dreaming of ways to make that person happy through special surprises, flowers, how they dress. They make mental notes of items they want to talk about and if there is a longer-than-usual separation, the anxiety is like an automatic burner set aflame. There is a great internal desire to be reunited as soon as possible.

In order not to be misunderstood, let me add that I'm aware there are two aspects to love. There must be commitment as well as emotion. There's an act of the will: "I choose to give my love to you, and to you exclusively." Christian marital love involves romance deepened by commitment. On those occasions when you don't feel romantic, the commitment stands, insuring the continuation of the union and a quick return of the emotions as well. These two aspects, feeling and pledging, work together. But we're centering on matters of the heart right now because that's the subject around which The Song of Solomon revolves. Let's briefly take this statement, "A characteristic of those in love is the desire to be in one another's presence," into the spiritual area.

Those who make up the Bride of Christ ought to want to spend time in their lover's presence. Do you look forward to extended sessions with the Lord through the course of a week? During a day do you often find yourself sharing expressions of your love with him? Do you joyously enter into the services of corporate worship at your church when the congregation expresses its appreciation of God? Even when your schedule is hectic and you aren't able through prayer and Scripture to be alone with God the way you might like, does this same automatic pilot begin to burn? "I really must get together again with my Lord very soon now."

If your answer to these or similar questions is *no*, a big part of your problem may be that you fail to realize the extent to which you are loved by God! If the one you say you care for has never been able to overwhelm you with the love he has for you, it's inevitable the relationship is going to break down sooner or later.

Let me share a glimpse of God's love as it's revealed in the Bible. This passage was chosen because it shows a little of the emotion he feels toward those to whom he's committed himself.

> When Israel was a child, I loved him, and out of Egypt I called my son. The more I called them, the more they went from me; they kept sacrificing to the Baals, and burning incense to idols.
>
> Yet it was I who taught Ephraim to walk, I took them up in my arms; but they did not know that I healed them. I led them with cords of compassion, with the bands of love, and I became to them as one who eases the yoke on their jaws, and I bent down to them and fed them.
>
> They shall return to the land of Eypgt, and Assyria shall be their king, because they have refused to return to me. The sword shall rage against their cities, consume the bars of their gates, and devour them in their fortresses.
>
> How can I give you up, O Ephraim! How can I hand you over, O Israel! . . . My heart recoils within me, my compassion grows warm and tender (Hos. 11:1-8).

You can hardly miss the affection, can you? I fear Christians tend to allow our commitment to God to so dominate our relationship that we fail to perceive the feelings he holds toward us. He truly cares for us! And for *you!*

Could it be you are so busy proving your commitment to God through so many acts that you can no longer just delight in his presence? Have your feelings of love died, or are they growing?

Let me refer again to the story *Fiddler on the Roof.* Tevya, the poor Russian Jewish dairyman, finds his world changing. Tradition is breaking down, and his daughters are marrying men of their own choice instead of the ones picked by the matchmaker. They talk now of "love," and he is confused by it all.

"Do you love me?" he asks his wife.

She replies, "Do I love you? With our daughter getting married, and trouble in the town. You're upset, you're worn out, go inside, go lie down. Maybe it's indigestion!

He persists, "Goldie, I'm asking you a question, do you love me?"

"You're a fool!" she snaps.

"I know, but do you love me?"

"Do I love you? For twenty-five years I've washed your clothes, cooked your meals, cleaned your house, given you children, milked the cow. After twenty-five years why talk about love right now?"

And that's the only way she can respond! Her relationship is one of commitment, but her feelings have become strictly functional.

Some of you need to know that God loves you with all his heart. In fact Song of Solomon 7:10 reads, "I am my beloved's, and his desire is for me!" The awareness of that kind of love needs to permeate your understanding. His desire is for you! My final desire is for you to be so captured by this realization that you can hardly wait until a rendevous is arranged to meet with him again.

A characteristic of those in love is the desire to be in one another's presence. If what I've said about God's feelings toward you is actually true, what are your feelings toward him? And might it not be wise to find time to meet with him today?